Mel Bay Presents

THE LIFE AND MUSIC OF AMY BEACH
THE FIRST WOMAN COMPOSER OF AMERICA

compiled and edited by Gail Smith

Acknowledgments

Kaye Burnett, Resident Director of the MacDowell Colony, Inc.

Marian Chase, Historical Society of Henniker, N.H.

Roland Goodbody, Special Collections Librarian, The University of New Hampshire (The Diary of Amy Beach 1941–44, and numerous letters in their collection)

Peter Munstedt, Conservatory Librarian, The University of Missouri–Kansas City (the original manuscripts of Amy written when she was 4, 10, and 11)

Lindsey E. Merrill (Mrs. H. H. A. Beach: Her Life and Music), The University of Rochester, Eastman School of Music, Ph.D., 1963

Robert Saladini, Music Specialist, The Library of Congress, Music Division, Washington, D.C.

Emma Yeaton Wheeler, former member of a Beach Club in New Hampshire (personal interview)

Selma Quick Youngdahl, copyist for Amy Beach (interviews and letters from Amy Beach)

The artist Lillian Bantz, interviewed prior to her death in October 1989 by the author

The photographs are used by permission of The University of New Hampshire, Special Collections.

Visit us on the Web at www.melbay.com — E-mail us at email@melbay.com

Contents

Acclaimed the **first woman composer of America**, Amy Beach composed the mighty "Gaelic Symphony," the "Piano Concerto in C♯ Minor," hundreds of choral, vocal, and chamber works, an opera, and numerous other works during her lifetime. In the process she encouraged other women composers of her day. She was a member of the National League of American Pen Women and ASCAP (American Society of Composers and Publishers). She served as leader of several organizations, including the Music Teachers National Association and the Music Educators National Conference. She was co-founder in 1926 and the first president of the Association of American Women Composers.

Amy Beach was a highly disciplined composer, capable of writing large-scale works in a matter of a few days. She was energetic in the promotion of her compositions, eagerly arranging for performances as soon as the works were finished. Equally gifted as a pianist, she had a virtuoso technique and an extraordinary memory. It is told of her that on one occasion she played the Schumann piano concerto with the Boston Orchestra at a week's notice, in place of a soloist who had canceled at the last moment!

This book contains many of her easier piano works, as well as intermediate to advanced pieces. The first four solos have never before been published. "Mamma's Waltz" was written when Amy was just 4 years old. The other three were written when she was only 10 or 11 years old.

Amy Beach said, "Pass on whatever joy you may discover in your work." It is my joy to pass on the following information on the life and music of **Amy Beach,** the first great woman composer of America.

Gail Smith

Amy Marcy Cheney.

Mrs. Henry Harris Aubrey Beach.

4

et's go back to the time when Amy Beach was born. The United States had just bought Alaska from Russia. The trans–Atlantic cable had just been laid, establishing lasting contact with Europe by wire. The term "impressionism" had just been coined by a journalist after viewing Monet's canvas called "Impressions."

Amy's parents were Clara Imogene (Marcy) and Charles Abbott Cheney. They were descendants of some of the earliest colonial New England families. Charles was educated at Phillips Exeter Academy and entered Bates College at the age of 16. He maintained a lifelong interest in mathematics while pursuing an active career, first in his father's papermaking business and later as a paper importer. From her father, Amy acquired much of his remarkable aptitude for languages and scholarly taste.

Amy's musical talents were inherited from her mother's family, who were all exceptionally interested in music. Her grandmother had an unusual soprano voice with a high range, and an aunt with a much-admired contralto voice was a prominent singer in local concerts. Chester Marcy, Amy's grandfather, was a fine clarinetist. Amy's mother, Clara Marcy, sang and played the piano, gave instruction, and appeared occasionally in concert.

Clara Imogene Cheney, Amy's mother.

Charles A. Cheney, Amy's father.

Amy Marcy Cheney was born in the little town of Henniker, New Hampshire, on September 5, 1867. When she was just 1 year old, she had memorized and could sing 40 different songs. She was gifted with perfect pitch and an accurate memory. Her bright, inquisitive nature constantly was alert for new information. By 17 months of age, she had associated sentences with her alphabet blocks and had learned the whole alphabet by herself. In a few weeks more, she was reciting nursery rhymes that had been read to her.

In a letter that Amy's mother wrote to Aunt Clara, she says, "Before two years of age she would, when being rocked to sleep in my arms, improvise a perfectly correct alto to any soprano air I might sing."

Amy's extremely sensitive nature made her upset at the sound of people laughing or at the sight of raindrops on the window. She would beg her mother to "wipe the tears." Music in the minor keys made her sad. No other punishment was needed for the little hands that occasionally were mischievous than for her mother to play Gottschalk's "Last Hope" on the piano.

When Amy was 3 years old, she could read very well. Her favorite story was Charles Dickens' "A Child's Dream of a Star." She began appearing regularly at her Sunday school concerts and recited psalms and poems, sometimes of considerable length; in one instance she recited a poem that was 13 minutes in length! Amy's Sunday school teacher was Miss Phillbrick at the Central Congregational Church in Chelsea, Massachusetts, and while in her class Amy also memorized all of Psalm 91, her favorite.

The birthplace of Amy Beach — Main St., West Henniker, New Hampshire.

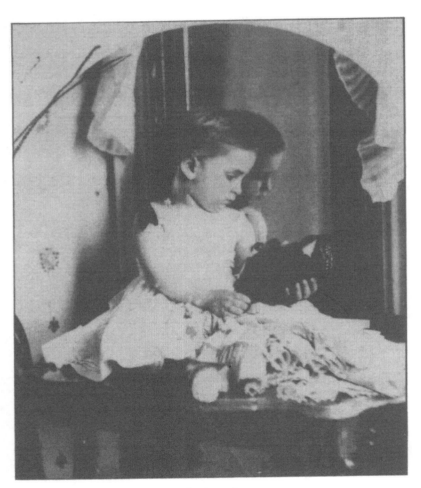

"Little Amy."

At this time Amy began showing her preferences for certain pieces of music that her mother played by designating it as the blue, pink, or purple music. Little attention was paid to this at first, because it was thought that she connected these colors with the color of the outside page of the publication. Afterwards it was very clearly demonstrated that the music played by her mother was not satisfactory to the child, because it did not correspond with a scheme of color that she had in **her** mind. When carefully questioned, it was discovered that the various colors corresponded with certain keys . . . a color for a key. She associated the following colors with the following keys, and they stayed that way all her life:

Blue ....A Flat
Green ....A
Pink ....E Flat
Violet ....D Flat
White C
Red ....G
Yellow ....E
Black ....F Sharp Minor or
                        G Sharp Minor

When she was 4 years old, Amy would play the hymn tunes she had heard at church, and play them with full harmony in their original keys. She would stand on a hassock at the piano and play a correct secondo part, improvising melodies unknown to her played as a primo by her aunt. In fact, it was difficult to keep her away from the piano.

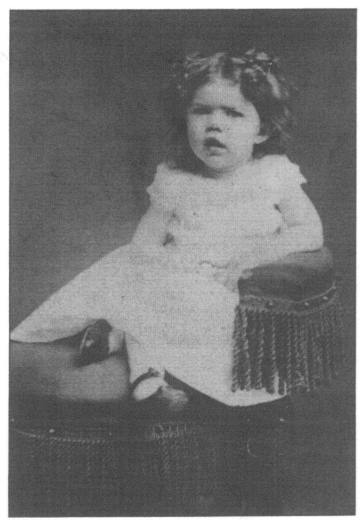

Amy as a "tiny tot."

Once while her mother was away, Amy stayed with her grandfather for six weeks. She enjoyed her visit in the country, listening to the birds sing and walking in the vast fields of flowers. During this time there was no piano around, so she composed a waltz in her mind. She played it for her mother when back home without an interruption. She had named it "Mamma's Waltz." Her mother wrote it down as she had played it. It is preserved and in the possession of the University of Missouri–Kansas City Library and used by their permission in this book.

When Amy was 5 years old she could read at sight, without instruction, playing and singing at the same time. At the age of 6 she could play by ear everything that she heard so far as the size of her hands would allow. Finally, her mother started giving her lessons three times a week.

At the age of 7 Amy made her first public appearance in concert at the Unitarian Church in Chelsea, Massachusetts. She played the Beethoven sonata "Opus No. 49," a Chopin waltz, Handel's "Harmonious Blacksmith," and her own waltz as an encore.

Amy as a young girl.

Amy's parents realized that they had a very precocious child and consulted with many experts as to where she should study music. The unanimous opinion was that she was qualified to enter any conservatory in Europe, but after considering various propositions they wisely decided to keep her at home for her general education.

When Amy was 8, her parents moved to Boston, where she was enrolled in a private school directed by W. L. Whittemore. There she especially enjoyed natural science, French, and German. Her piano instruction was continued by Ernst Perabo and later by Junius W. Hill and Carl Baermann. In the winter of 1881–1882, Hill gave her a course in harmony, the only formal instruction in music theory she ever received.

In the last years of her life, Amy spoke of this period of her childhood: "Managers came to my parents, offering anything for this tot who could play... in addition to Beethoven, Handel, and Chopin ... her own compositions, this infant prodigy. But Father and Mother, guided by a divine instinct, refused them all ... these contracts so tempting to a young couple. They knew that early aggrandizement must be harmful to their nervous, delicate child, and they had decided that I was to grow up just like any other little one, adopting music as a profession when I was old enough."*

Amy's home in Boston at 28 Commonwealth Avenue.

*From "How Music Is Made," *Keyboard* winter issue, 1942.

At the age of 10, Amy wrote two lovely pieces, "Romanza" and "Menuetta." "Petit Valse" was written as a Christmas present to her aunt a year later.

Amy was then asked to do a very interesting and exciting thing, all because she had absolute pitch. Professor Edward R. Sill took Amy to the fields in California to hear the various birds and then notate on paper the songs the birds sang. He especially wanted her to hear the California lark. This was considered a great contribution to ornithological science and was put in a scientific paper by a colleague.

Amy continued these observations all her life and wrote many songs based on the actual songs of birds, such as "The Hermit Thrush at Morn" (Op. 92, No. 2), "The Hermit Thrush at Eve" (Op. 92, No. 1), and "The Humming Bird" (Op. 128, No. 3).

The hermit thrush *catharus guttatus* is considered to be the finest songbird because of its flute-like song. The exact song of this bird was notated by Amy as she heard it singing outside her studio at the MacDowell Colony one summer that she was in residence there.

On October 24, 1883, at the age of 16, Amy made her first public appearance in Boston as a concert pianist. She played Ignaz Moscheles' G minor concerto "Opus 60" with orchestra and Chopin's "Rondo" in E flat as a solo. "On that occasion the aged widow of Moscheles, having heard of the remarkable young girl's work, sent her a most cordial letter of congratulation which also gave several very interesting facts about the concerto as well as other compositions of her famous husband."*

During that winter season, she gave several recitals and, at the age of 17, played the Chopin F minor concerto with the Boston Symphony Orchestra under the direction of Wilhelm Gericke on March 28, 1885. The critic of the *Boston Evening Transcript* was impressed with her "thoroughly artistic, beautiful and brilliant performance," commenting that she played "with a totality of conception that one seldom finds in players of her sex."

During the summer of that year, Amy was taken to Dr. H. H. A. Beach for treatment of a sore finger. Dr. Beach was a widower and 24 years older than Amy. He was a member of the Harvard medical faculty and had been associated with Dr. Oliver Wendell Holmes in his lectures on practical anatomy. Dr. Beach began his medical career in hospital work during the Civil War while yet a student at Harvard. At the close of the war he received an appointment to the Massachusetts General Hospital, where after many years of service he became consulting surgeon. Dr. Beach was an accomplished pianist and very interested in the arts.

Amy married Dr. H. H. A. Beach on December 2, 1885, in Boston's Trinity Church. She was just 18 years old.

Amy as a teenager. She often appeared in concerts with a long braid down her back.

Amy as a young woman.

*Gertrude F. Cowen quoted in *The Musical Courier* in her article "Mrs. H. H. A. Beach, the Celebrated Composer."

From her wedding day on, Amy wore her long hair on top of her head in a bun. During her 25 years of marriage, she would compose the majority of her works. Because of Dr. Beach's wealth and position, all of her appearances from the time of her marriage until her husband's death were for some charity or cause.

Her husband opposed formal study in composition for her. He thought it would rob her work of its originality and freedom. He encouraged her to continue studying by herself.

She began translating from French the musical treatises of Berlioz and Francois Gevaert. She studied fugue by writing out from memory much of Bach's *Well-Tempered Clavichord* and compared her version with Bach's. Similarly, she taught herself orchestration. She said, "I worked very hard for years. I possess about every treatise that has ever been written on the subject of harmony, theory, counterpoint, double counterpoint, fugue, and instrumentation. I have a large library of these books. . . . I wrote out scores of Beethoven from memory, and then would take my work next day and compare it with the playing of the orchestra."*

Her first published work was "The Rainy Day" (1880), a setting of Longfellow's well-known poem, issued in 1883 by Oliver Ditson Publishing Company. Next came another set of songs, a cadenza to Beethoven's C minor concerto, and "Valse Caprice" for piano. But "Opus 5," which was begun the year following her marriage, was a Mass in E flat major for vocal quartet, chorus, orchestra, and organ which required three whole years to complete. This was an ambitious undertaking for any composer. It was first performed by the Handel and Haydn Society with the Boston Symphony Orchestra on February 7, 1892. This was a first . . . before this time the group had never performed a work composed by a woman!

Dr. and Mrs. H. H. A. Beach soon after their marriage.

Piano Mastery, Second Series by Harriette Brower, pg. 186, "Talks with Master Pianists and Teachers."

Amy's popularity was growing both in the United States and abroad. News came from Sweden that a group of her songs had been performed in concert in the Royal Palace. The King expressed a deep interest in all the compositions written by Mrs. Beach.

Her position as the most prominent American woman composer of her time was confirmed in 1892 by a commission to write a work for the dedication of the Woman's Building at the World's Columbian Exposition in Chicago. She composed "Festival Jubilate" (Op. 17) for chorus and orchestra. Dr. and Mrs. Beach travelled to this exciting event and Dr. Beach, beaming with pride, said to a friend, "I am quite content to be a tail to her kite."

Her next work was probably the most important of her career. It was the "Gaelic Symphony," which was completed in the spring of 1896. It was first performed in October by the Boston Symphony Orchestra under the direction of Emil Paur and was subsequently played in New York, Brooklyn, Buffalo, Kansas City, San Francisco, and Chicago. In the six weeks following its completion, she wrote a sonata in A minor for violin and piano (Op. 34).

In March of 1898, Amy Beach appeared in a program featuring her own works as a benefit for the Elizabeth Peabody House in Boston. She and Olive Mead, violinist, played several of her works for piano and violin, including "Romance" (Op. 23). The program also included the song "Forget-me-not" to words by Dr. Beach.

In June 1898 came the premiere of another commissioned choral work, "Song of Welcome," written to open the Trans–Mississippi Exposition in Omaha.

Amy pictured in a black beaded dress.

13

On April 7, 1900, Amy Beach appeared .with the Boston Symphony in the premiere of her "Piano Concerto in C Sharp Minor" (Opus 45). This was her last big orchestral work.

In an interview published in *The Etude* Magazine in 1904, a vivid picture is given of the composer. She was then in her mid-30s. William Armstrong said, "She is a woman of charmingly simple manners. . . . She is of medium height. Her eyes are of a grayish blue, large and smiling. Her complexion is fresh and brilliant. Her blonde hair, primly parted, is brushed back smoothly from her face. The manner of her wearing it and the quaint style of her dress . . . make her appear older than she in reality is."

Dr. and Mrs. Beach had a summer home in Centerville, on Cape Cod, that she bought with the proceeds of her composition "Ecstasy" (Op. 19), written in 1893. Her husband built this home for her, and Amy loved it. She asked a young artist to do a painting of it . . . the drawing became her Christmas greeting card.

On June 28, 1910, Dr. H. H. A. Beach died. He and Amy had almost reached their 25th wedding anniversary. It had been a happy marriage and, even as the years went by, she celebrated her wedding anniversary in her heart. In her diary on December 2, 1943, she wrote that it was her "58th Anniversary"!

Her mother died almost at the same time as Amy's husband. Amy had little heart left to continue her beautiful work; but, realizing her husband would have wanted her to go on, she decided that a complete change of scene would be good.

On September 5, 1911 (her 44th birthday), she set sail for Europe. After some rest, she began giving concerts in Hamburg, Leipzig, Berlin, and numerous other cities. The press and public greeted her with warmth, enthusiasm, and deep appreciation for her creative gifts.

This is the Christmas card Amy Beach sent out with her home pictured on it. The home was drawn by Lillian Bantz, who was a young artist living in the area at the time.

Amy enjoyed playing her piano concerto with the great orchestras of Europe. She stayed almost four years, returning in 1914 at the outbreak of World War I.

When she returned to America, she had adopted a more modern style of dress and coiffure, and she resumed her concert career. With 30 concerts booked, she traveled across the country performing her works. Her "Panama Hymn" was accepted by the Panama–Pacific Exposition as its official hymn. In 1915 she moved to New York. Thereafter, she spent winters on tour and summers practicing or composing.

Beginning in 1921, she went to the MacDowell Colony in Peterborough, New Hampshire, to compose. Many of her compositions were written there during 15 different summer visits. In fact, her last chamber work, "Piano Trio" (Op. 150), was written in just three days there during the summer of 1938. She became a good friend of Marian MacDowell, the founder of the MacDowell Colony. The Colony is the 420-acre former estate of Edward MacDowell. There private studios are scattered among the secluded woods that afford complete peace and privacy. Amy Beach always stayed in the Watson Studio when she was there.

Marian MacDowell was a fine pianist and gave concerts of her late husband's works. When she was 97 years old, she wrote to the director of the MacDowell Colony, wanting to finish raising a $10,000 fellowship "in honor of Mrs. Beach who was a fine composer and the first woman composer ever to get universal recognition."*

Amy returned to Europe again in 1929 to play a benefit concert at the American Embassy in Rome. While there, she finished her "String Quartet" (Op. 89).

American Composers' Day, 1915. Amy Beach is holding a bouquet of flowers at the Panama–Pacific Exposition. The posters in the background read "American Composers' Day" and "Organ Recitals 10 Cents."

Amy Beach at the Watson Studio, the MacDowell Colony, Peterborough, New Hampshire

---

*From a letter in the MacDowell collection at the Library of Congress in Washington, D.C., dated October 6, 1954, from Marian MacDowell to Carlton Smith.

During Amy Beach's lifetime, numerous Beach Clubs sprang up all over the country. Usually the piano teacher of a town organized one with her students and was then affiliated with the Federation of Music Clubs. There was one such club in Amy Beach's hometown. Often she would play for this special group. The club sent their picture along with a story of their club to a national magazine.

The adjacent article and picture are a reprint from *The Etude* Magazine, April 1924. In the top row, the first girl on the left with the large bow in her hair is Emma Yeaton Wheeler of Milford, New Hampshire. She had the unique privilege of hearing Mrs. Beach play the piano in person when she was a little girl in the local Beach Club. She also rode in the car when her father (who had the only car in town) drove Mrs. Beach to the MacDowell Colony. On one occasion, Mrs. Beach gave Emma a beautiful amethyst pin and necklace she was wearing.

THE ETUDE

Mrs. H. H. A. Beach Sets an Example

EVERYBODY realizes the great work done by musical clubs in America. The need for activity in the musical club field is not nearly so much with the adult who employs the music club at times as a kind of social pasture in which to get away from the problems of business or the home, as it is for the child who is just beginning to get an acquaintance with music. Mrs. H. H. A. Beach, who doubtless ranks as the greatest living composer of her sex and is certainly one of the comparatively few "great" American composers, has found time and enthusiasm to assist in many ways a club formed in her honor in her home, at Hillsboro, N. H. THE ETUDE has made it a more or less strict rule not to publish pictures of clubs, because we have so many hundreds of applications to do so that we can not accommodate all. But the instance of an extremely busy woman, standing at the top of her profession, finding time to promote the interests of a children's club is so noteworthy that we desire to call Mrs. Beach's example to the attention of others. Do not say that you are "too busy to form a children's music club." If you really want to do it you will find a way. The following report of the activities of the club coming from one of its supporters will be interesting to our readers:

To THE ETUDE:

Here we are! The Beach Club, of Hillsboro, New Hampshire, and the happiest group of children in the whole State. We had this picture of ourselves taken on purpose to give to our dear Mrs. Beach, for a Christmas present.

We are very proud of our Beach Club, and think we have reason to be, for we are the only Federated Juvenile Music Club in New Hampshire. And then, as Mrs. H. H. A. Beach, the most noted woman composer in America, lives in Hillsboro, we have her present at all our meetings.

We all love Mrs. Beach; she is so jolly and kind to us; we are not a bit afraid to play before her. She seems to enjoy it and then she always plays for us.

As we are too young and do not play well enough to belong to the grown-up Music Club, our piano teachers helped us to organize the Beach Club. There are nearly thirty members in all; and most of us are under twelve years of age. We have one drummer, a violinist, and a singer; all the rest play the piano.

We have officers just like the grown-up club. When we elected our first president by ballot, some of the boys voted for themselves. They said afterwards, they really wanted Marguerite, but did not know how to spell her name. The president we have now can not talk plain, but she is very dignified and we never think of whispering.

After the business part of the meeting is over, the president announces our names and each one tells the name of his piece and its composer. Some of the names are hard to pronounce, but we have to learn to say them correctly. We do not sit in the room with the piano; but when Mrs. Beach plays she lets us all stand around her.

One day we had a Bach and Beach program and one of the boys, knowing that Mrs. Beach would be at the meeting, asked his mother if Bach would be there, too. He knows better, now, for in December we gave a Bach play and learned many things about him. We played some of Bach's music and Mrs. Beach played two pieces of his she learned when just a little girl. There is a whole book of these plays written by Mr. James Francis Cooke. We are glad, for we think it is more fun to act plays than to read about the composers.

We wish all children could have a Beach Club, and of course they can, but there is only one Mrs. Beach and she belongs to us.

LISABEL GAY

THE BEACH CLUB

If Mrs. H. H. A. Beach, the most distinguished woman in American music and also one of the busiest, can take time to foster a musical club, should not others follow her example and fine initiative? There are hundreds of clubs like this in various parts of the country. Unfortunately this one picture must remain as the prototype of many, many similar pictures simply because THE ETUDE has not room to print such pictures regularly. The Young Folk's Musical Clubs are the real foundation of all American musical club activity. Why not follow Mrs. Beach's example and found a club?

M rs. Beach was responsible for helping many young artists along in their careers. One such artist was Miss Ruth Shaffner, who she heard at St. Bartholomew's Church in New York City. She was singing the soprano solo in the composer's "Magnificat." Her voice greatly impressed Mrs. Beach, who began to write songs for her. They began performing together, including a command performance at the White House for First Lady Eleanor Roosevelt.

A picture of First Lady Eleanor Roosevelt, inscribed: "To dear Mrs. Beach with appreciation & good wishes. Eleanor Roosevelt."

Amy had a woman copy her manuscripts for her before sending them to her publishers. In one letter to her she states, "My dear Mrs. Quick: You must be wondering why you have not heard from me after I had written to you in the Autumn. When that letter went to you I was feeling at my best, working hard and fully expecting to send you something to copy before many weeks. Two days from that time I was on the operating table, most unexpectedly. Fortunately all went well but it has taken me a long time to regain strength and naturally work has had to be put one side. I am not to be allowed any concert work this winter but later I hope to be able to finish, at least a few of the brief sketches which I was able to gather during those few days at the MacDowell Colony. . . ."*

Always a devout Episcopalian, Mrs. Beach wrote a considerable amount of church music, anthems, contatas, "Te Deum in F," a Communion service, the "Canticle of the Sun," and the cantata "Christ in the Universe" (Op. 133). The very last composition she produced, "Though I Take the Wings of Morning" (Op. 152), is also sacred.

On March 15, 1932, the Federated Music Club sponsored a special program presenting the works of Amy Beach by a hook-up of radio stations throughout the country. On May 8, 1940, Mrs. Beach was honored at a dinner in New York's Town Hall Club, attended by some 200 composers, musicians, and friends. Marian MacDowell, the composer Douglas Moore, and pianist Olga Samaroff were among those who paid warm tribute to her.

In 1942, to celebrate Amy's 75th birthday, Elena de Sayn, a violinist and critic from Washington, D.C., organized two concerts of Amy's music.

Mrs. H. H. A. Beach died of heart disease in New York City at 5:00 p.m., December 27, 1944. She had been ill for six weeks. She was 77 years old.

*From a letter from Amy Beach to Mrs. Selma Quick Youngdahl dated February 28, 1937.

Amy Beach at her summer home in Centerville, Cape Cod.

This picture was taken March 19, 1940, and sent to Amy Beach with a note that said, "A little souvenir of your visit to the Brooklyn Chamber Music Society."

MRS. BEACH DEAD; COMPOSER, PIANIST

One of America's Best Known Women Musicians Stricken In Hotel Suite Here at 77

Mrs. H. H. A. Beach, most celebrated of American women composers, who produced eighty numbered works and the musical settings for 150 songs, died yesterday in her suite in the Hotel Barclay, 111 East Forty-eighth Street, after a six weeks illness of heart disease. She was 77 years old.

The composer was born at Henniker, N. H., a daughter of Charles Abbott Cheney and the former Clara Imogene Marcy, and inherited from her mother, a pianist and singer, much of her musical talent. When only 4 years old she began to write little musical compositions which were always characterized by a pretty "tune" and gave evidence of inventive powers.

She studied pianoforte with Ernst Perabo and Carl Baermann of Boston, but in theory and composition she made her way almost entirely without aid or supervision. She was exceedingly careful and thorough, tireless in application to the end of her active career.

Made Debut at 16

At 16 Mrs. Beach made her public debut as a pianist, playing the Moschelas G minor concerto in the Music Hall, Boston. The next year she played Chopin's F minor concerto with the Boston Symphony Orchestra under Gericke, and the Mendelssohn D minor concerto with the Theodore Thomas Orchestra. In 1886 she began the composition of her first important work, the Mass in E flat, for solo voices, chorus, orchestra and organ, which she finished three years later. It was presented in 1892 by the Handel and Haydn Society of Boston with a vocal quartet; the first time the society, the oldest music organization in the United States, produced a work by a woman.

That same year she became the first woman to have her name appear on the program of the New York Symphony Society as a composer. Walter Damrosch was the conductor. In 1893 Theodore Thomas presented in Chicago her "Festival Jubilate" for chorus and orchestra.

MRS. H. H. A. BEACH

Mamma's Waltz

Written at age four

Amy Marcy Cheney
(1877)

A tempo

rit.

23

Menuetto

Written at age ten

Amy Marcy Cheney
(1877)

Romanza

Composed in 1877
When Amy was ten years old

Amy Marcy Cheney
(1877)

Petit Valse

Written when Amy was eleven

Amy Marcy Cheney
(1878)

29

Pierrot and Pierrette

Written in 1894

Mrs. H.H. A. Beach,
Op. 25, No. 4

Waltz

Mrs. H.H. A. Beach,
Op. 36, No. 3

Cantabile

33

Minuet in F

Mrs. H.H. A. Beach,
Op. 36, No. 1

Harlequin

Mrs. H.H. A. Beach,
Op. 25, No. 6

Canoeing

Tranquillo e sempre legato

Mrs. H. H. A. Beach,
Op. 119, No. 3

41

Secrets

Mrs. H.H. A. Beach,
Op. 25, No. 5

43

The Returning Hunter

Mrs. H.H. A. Beach,
Op. 64, No. 2

Gavotte

48

Sliding On The Ice

Mrs. H.H. A. Beach,
Op. 119, No. 1

Gavotte Fantastique

Mrs. H.H. A. Beach,
Op. 54, No. 2

Scottish Legend

Mrs. H.H.A. Beach,
Op. 54, No. 1

60

Menuet Italien

Allegretto con delicatezza

Mrs. H.H. A. Beach,
Op. 28, No. 2

Fire - Flies

Mrs. H.H. A. Beach

70

In Autumn

("Feuillages jaunissants sur les gazons épars.")

Lamartine

Mrs. H. H. A. Beach

78

Summer Dreams

By
Mrs. H.A.A. Beach

Duets

The Brownies

"Through the house give glimmering light,
By the dead and drowsy fire:
Every elf and fairy sprite
Hop as light as bird from brier."

Shakespeare.

Mrs. H.H. A. Beach,
Op. 47, No. 1

Secondo

82

The Brownies

"Through the house give glimmering light,
By the dead and drowsy fire:
Every elf and fairy sprite
Hop as light as bird from brier."

Shakespeare.

Mrs. H.H. A. Beach,
Op. 47, No. 1

83

Secondo
85

Secondo

Robin Redbreast

"In country lanes the robins sing,
Clear-throated, joyous, swift of wing,
From misty dawn to dewy eve
(Though cares of nesting vex and grieve)
Their little heart-bells ring and ring."

C.H. Lüders.

Mrs. H.H. A. Beach,
Op. 47, No. 2

Tempo di valse   **Secondo**

Robin Redbreast

(a.) For the first eight measures this melody reproduces exactly the song of a robin, heard during an entire summer. The beauty of tone and perfection of rhythmic accent suggested the performance of an accomplished flute-player.

(b.) This melodic variation was occasionally introduced by the bird, but the key never changed.

(c.) The song of the "Chewink," or "Ground-Robin".

Mrs. H.H. A. Beach,
Op. 47, No. 2

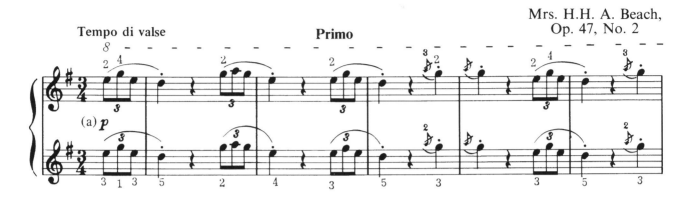

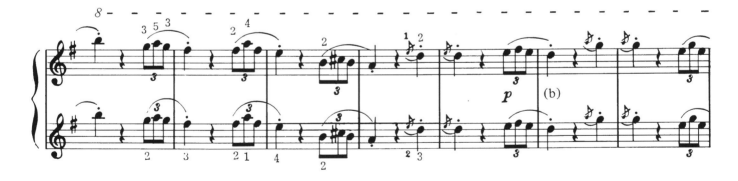

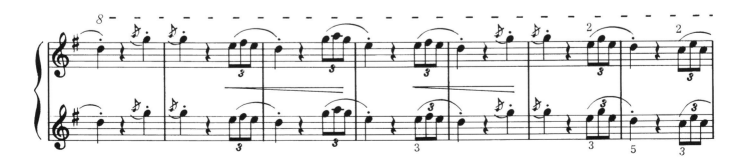

Primo

Twilight

"The birds have hushed themselves to rest,
And night comes fast, to drop her pall
Till morn brings life to all".

H.H.A.B.

Mrs. H.H. A. Beach,
Op. 47, No. 3

Secondo

Largo religioso

94

Twilight

"The birds have hushed themselves to rest,
And night comes fast, to drop her pall
Till morn brings life to all".

H.H.A.B.

Mrs. H. H. A. Beach,
Op. 47, No. 3

Primo

95

Katy-dids

"The katy-did works her chromatic reed
on the walnut tree over the well".

Whitman.

Mrs. H.H. A. Beach,
Op. 47, No. 4

Secondo

Katy-dids

"The katy-did works her chromatic reed
on the walnut tree over the well".

Whitman.

Primo

Mrs. H.H. A. Beach,
Op. 47, No. 4

Elfin Tarantelle

"Fairies, black, gray, green, and white,
You moonshine revellers, and shades of night".
Shakespeare.

Secondo

Mrs. H.H. A. Beach,
Op. 47, No. 5

Elfin Tarantelle

"Fairies, black, gray, green, and white,
You moonshine revellers, and shades of night".
Shakespeare.

Primo

Mrs. H.H. A. Beach,
Op. 47, No. 5

Allegro molto

Secondo

102

Primo

Secondo

Primo

105

Good Night

"Goodnight! The crimson scented rose
Droops low her pretty head,
And the little grasses long ago
Their evening prayers have said.

Night's starry eyes are blinking
At the moonbeams silvery light,
While the lily hides her golden heart
And whispers soft, - "Goodnight."
Agnes Helen Lockhart.

Secondo

Mrs. H. H. A. Beach,
Op. 47, No. 6

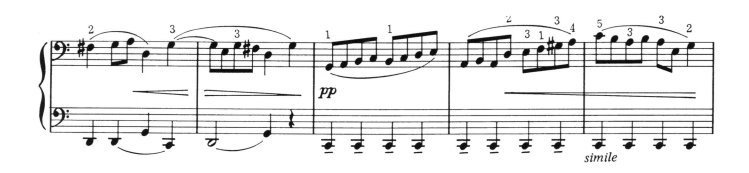

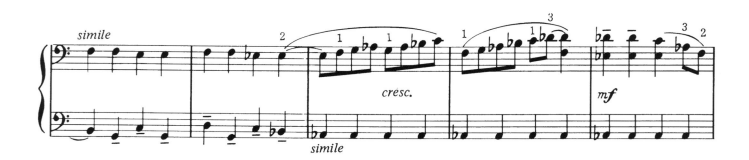

Good Night

"Goodnight!" The crimson scented rose
Droops low her pretty head,
And the little grasses long ago
Their evening prayers have said.

Night's starry eyes are blinking
At the moonbeams silvery light,
While the lily hides her golden heart
And whispers soft,-"Goodnight."

Agnes Helen Lockhart.

Mrs. H.H. A. Beach,
Op. 47, No. 6

Primo

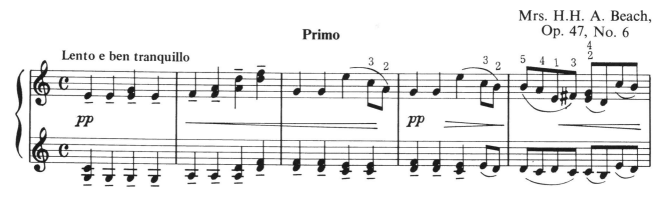

Secondo

Primo

109

Made in the USA
San Bernardino, CA
11 December 2013